Murmur & Crush

Murmur
& Crush

Maya Janson

Cover image © Adam Fuss
Courtesy Cheim & Read, New York

Author photo by Margaret Babbott

Printed and published by
Hedgerow Books/Levellers Press
Amherst, Massachusetts

ISBN 978-1-937146-18-4

CONTENTS

I

II

III

The following poems have appeared in these publications:

Salamander: "Lying on a Hill Under Stars."

Prairie Schooner: "Field Notes from a State of Well-being" and "Calling the Whiskey Roses."

Harvard Review and *Best American Poetry 2000:* "Considering the Demise of Everything."

Many Mountains Moving: "Driving Home from the Zendo."

The Alaska Quarterly Review: "Trying to Locate the Beginning."

Jubilat: "That Which In Us Rises To Be Sung To."

Barrow Street: "The Use of Sorrow to Overcome Sorrow."

The Poetry Miscellany: "Letter Written in this Life, Mailed from the Next."

Third Coast: "We Dedicate this Practice" and "Murmur" (as "Everyone Loves a Good Downpour").

Lyric: "1,000 Cranes" and "Poem with a Shaft of Light Running Through It."

Rattle: "Sky Stays the Same."

Green Mountains Review: "So Much Potentially Lost in Transmission."

Emprise Review: "It's Not the Last Remaining Bird."

Tupelo Press Poetry Project: "This is the final day of years of sweetness." (Petrarch 314)

The Collagist: "Disturbed Cirrus."

The Massachusetts Review: "Forged."

For John, for Orielle

June bug versus hurricane

— Lucinda Williams

I

Slow Drink from Abandoned Well

Start with Sault St. Marie at dusk,
the Precambrian shield tilting and shifting

under the weight of the continent, whole
sections of skyline in bad repair, like her heart.

His more like the threat of rain.
Alfalfa field in a downpour, hired men

running towards a barn minus their shirts,
tractor left to hiss in green and yellow, wavering.

Or the part of the Missouri they crossed
with a grain-man, red bluffs then two days

on the side of the road in a neglected pasture,
waiting for a ride. Waiting and braiding each other's

hair. They made of themselves a slack rope
in a field as dark came on and again leaning

against a tree. Years later arguing over the name
of the tree. Quince or pear.

They drank from an abandoned well
the kind of happiness that would travel

a great distance just to play its harmonica
with its boots kicked off humming

Me and Bobby McGee. Years later they agree
it was a little like watching a thunderhead

build its case all day over the grassland.
Not knowing if the stakes would hold

in tornadic winds. Not knowing what was at stake
or if desire's team of draft horses, yoked

and driven hard over the hills in the dark
would survive that which would blind them.

We are blind and then the rain stops. The rain
stops but the tendency to confuse love with morning

doesn't. Each day birds waking up in branches,
coming-to in a crush of something gone wild

in an orchard that is laden, obviously trying
to hold its own although stunned with blossom.

Sky Stays the Same

Coincidentally, the same summer the gazelles jumped
the fence at the ecotarium most of my married friends
were having affairs. We think we can
but we cannot contain the heart.
We continue to give it our best shot
like the nurse saying roll up your sleeve.
The inoculation is planted but there is no cure
for the who you are and what you want.
Now even my mother seems to have forgotten
the early years when she held me by a window
as it snowed and three deer came out of the woods
to stand blinking and pawing: the way I do
before the mural painted on the building downtown,
Sojourner Truth marching with clouds,
the clouds anonymous in their lab coats.
It's always the same sky, it's just the weather
and the seasons that keep changing.
In spring I dust the pollen from my hands,
then the maples along the river begin to smolder
in their red coronas. Dry days.
I've got an unquenchable thirst and can't sleep
because there's such a whirring of wings.
Such thievery in the orchard, so many
boxes of fruit hoisted over the back gate
long after the workers have climbed down
from their ladders, the smoke from their tobacco
lingering long after they've gone home for the day.

It's Not the Last Remaining Bird

getting the last word in at dusk.
It's not a word. With so much talk about
the coming of the end
it's hard to know where to begin.
I've lost all interest
in being smart or charming
and only want to stop
mid-path, lay down
in the grass and listen to the wind
boss the trees around.
Neither happiness nor unhappiness.
Nor the beveled place in a Levis poem
where a cat lay on the counter
of a rural post office or how
its fur stirred when a hand passed
over its sleeping body
when mailing a letter. Like the ones
we used to write to each other
in what seems now like another life.
Dear you, dear me.
When we lived in orchards.
When we slept in open fields.
When on a Canadian back road
there was so little traffic
we stretched out on the asphalt
as night fell, trying to
hold onto the day's heat,
saying here's a good thing,
here's a good thing a little longer.

Disturbed Cirrus

When I changed my name to water it was water over
the dam. No going back to the cold water flat; unheated
the pipes burst. When you left. When you years later
and out of the blue called to say just one last thing.
My love for you is the horse, not tractor,
pulling a plow in the field along the interstate.
Neither animal nor driver having any regard for the sky,
not even late in the day with the work of high ladders over.
Everything in balance then out of balance, falling
like the strand of hair that would never stay tucked.
Like the old man on that beach years ago north of Gander,
tucking his oars into the row boat, coming ashore
in the almost dark. It was dark and then it got darker.
What light remained came from his hands against the boat's
black hull. White like vapor over a caldera, small
like horses viewed from a distance, lost to the withers
in blonde grass. His fishing nets improbably filled
with fragile glass balls, the glass thick and pocked
like moon glass. Like glass fired in the moon's big kiln.
Look at us, all these years later still marked
as if by spilled ink. The whales at night
disappeared into the ink-spot sea and still we waited
on the beach for their return. We waited
on the beach, in our own way echolocating each other.
Later we lashed everything we owned into a pickup truck
with a good radio but without a working heater.
But without became what we whistled, picking blackberries
by a river upstate, *but without* while the sun crashed its plane
into the hills. They were hills, not mountains.
Their heads were bowed and they were big-shouldered
but their summits were not lost, didn't even
come close to touching the clouds.

This is the final day of years of sweetness
(Petrarch 314)

Think of straw. Fields of it. Then recall Edward's hair.
His temper. No trouble remembering

The last time you heard from him:
A phone call from a fishing boat in Alaska.

He was everything you wanted then he wasn't.
The kind of love that could cause you to lie down

In a field during a thunderstorm praying to be struck.
Matches in your pocket with the warning:

Close before striking. Bad love
Being better than no love at all.

The color of his hair, the final day in a year of sweetness.
It was pride of lions yellow, the animals sunning

And licking each other as a sign of filial devotion.
On the savannah in long grass. The savannah being

Long on grass but short on shade.
What trees there were were like an afterthought,

The lord saying oh yeah, let there be shade.
You can put all your trust in the lord your god

And still wake up in a field of straw too late
In the season to be harvested.

The field flooded after torrential rain.
The boy long gone.

Considering The Demise Of Everything

What if the 5:30 train shaking the trees at the edge of the woodlot—
What if the yellow flowers blooming in the swamp—
What if I can't find what I'm looking for?
Then thank you. Thank you water and pen, bell and candle.
Thank you rope, your coarse length lowers me
into the mineshaft. Cobalt and copper and diamond.
Thanks for the hammer. And the canary.
The bird is grateful for the opportunity to sing,
its yellow feathers fluffed at the neck.
Its song a bituminous flame, like a match
struck deep in a cavern. Is that water ahead?
Is that a ladder? Thank you for the cross-hatched
sky and the days I was able to
lie down under it with the man I loved.
What if it's summer and the clouds are gondolas?
What if I'm led beside still waters and cannot rest?
My head on his chest, looking up at the sky
while he combs the bangs off my forehead.
The sky is a handpainted clock.
Sometimes sun, sometimes moon.
The cross-hatching is accomplished by the terminal
ends of branches. It's the library lawn.
It's the town square of a small southwestern city.
Two old men playing checkers in the gradual dark.
Speaking Spanish across the courtyard: *rampido rampido*.
Who will translate? We are done with traveling.
We're hot and the last time we bathed was two states ago,
a creek just after sunrise. We're so thirsty.
And nothing is better than this water, this canteen.
This drinking.

Entertaining Larks

If I'd practiced my cello that could be me not Ma
holding its polished body between spread legs.
My velvet dress hiked up. Me & my trouble
sitting still channeled into enthusiastic
swaying & bowing. Unlike the lake in the woods
which has mastered staying put especially now
at the tag-end of winter when it looks like a catarac'd
eye. Eye of the giant. Eye of everything that broods me
while I caper in my hot-pink thrift store coat
tripping on upended roots of hemlock & witch hazel
while the dog wanders off after quail.
I give myself wholeheartedly to the entertainment of larks.
Maybe I'll be discovered. Finally visit Berlin.
On a regular basis I revisit the memory of the man,
the stranger on the Blue Line who asked me
from the barracks of his old world wool to give him
my hand in marriage. His gold rings cool on my wrist.
I was seventeen. I was reading Collette, I was reading
Willa Cather, my mind in a Parisian gutter,
my mind a prairie away. I was extinguishing
my Gauloise, I was chasing voles from the roof
of my sod house using nothing more than bare hands
and the business end of my homemade broom.

On the Anniversary Of

Start every conversation with a weather event.
End-of-the-world rain, nimbus and strata-something clouds

doing cartwheels over the alfalfa field, wind cruising
the streets of yourself in a beat up car with bald tires.

Start every poem with a statement of fact.
The price of butter in Russia, the scientific name of the lark.

Start every argument with a question. Why not?
After seeing a photograph of sea-grass shivering ecstatically

find your Schwinn and start biking down empty lanes, each one
leading to the bay, the water visible through slats of white fence,

baby doll heads of dahlias drooping. Of peonies peeking.
Everything is everything but there's not a blade of grass in sight.

Start every ending with a glance back over your shoulder.
Then bring in coyote, looking ragged, hungry.

Give him superpowers, have him watch you while you nap
in the great pasture, in full sunlight,

honeybees doing their bee dance, making
a dizzying crown around your head.

Though the Garden is Stockpiling Beetles

The rose maintains its posture of durable bliss.
Likewise, one glance across the breakfast table—
we prop each other up. We hold fast, sweep around
cobwebs, place exclamation points where needed.
The pelvic cradle rendered as a figure eight—
two joined loops that if broken become eyes
staring from a great darkness. The crows,
the summer you were twelve, endlessly
cawed in the salt marsh while your father, holed-up,
filled spiral notebooks with sketches of the human
figure, interlocking ovals that looked like smoke
signals sent from a fire that burned, yes,
but on a hill at some remove. Meanwhile,
in the house next door someone is always crying
or scolding the baby for trying to build a better
world out of unbuttered toast. Some kind of
decorous and wild lament. Floribunda, vena cava,
runaway bunny. In spite of everything,
do you still possess an unbridled love for the world?
Or are you like the doves in the mural downtown,
a shade of blue becoming by degrees whiter, moving
to the far corner and when you think no one is looking,
you fly away?

Calling the Whiskey Roses

It's always afternoon, you're
dragging a wooden chair across the kitchen
like a hunter with the carcass of a kill.
Hauled to the edge of the forest.

Chair wedged in the doorway
between two rooms, you begin to drink.
Tainted sunlight. Head tipped back,
the gold in your mouth, burning.

Then the slowed withdrawal,
mouth gone slack around the bottle.
The loosening of the throat,
each link of the chain you swallowed.

Then your hand reaching for the radio;
its small glow an ignited coal.
The easy slide of the dial.
Any music at all.

The Use of Sorrow to Overcome Sorrow

Sometimes it's impossible to hear the music.
No amount of amplification changes this fact.
By late winter our love is stacked cordwood

and we're running out. No amount of multiplication.
But when you're beside me, resting as after
a hard climb to a hill's summit, the view is unrivalled.

The world is a tossed kerchief, filled with wind.
A magician's box, a bamboo cage,
two white birds huddled beneath a cloth.

At least once a day I consider I may not be able
to make it. Not another step. Already I miss the bay,
people running toward the pier yelling *the blues*

are running, the blues. Meaning fish.
Baby at the window waving bye-bye.
Rain entering the river in small hatchet cuts.

Chop chop chop. The rain enters a river.
Sometimes there is too much remembrance.
The heart swells, becomes too big for its cavity.

It's like listening to sad fiddle music as fog lifts
over a slaked mountain, copper ore rolled out
on shaky carts. In the black and white photograph

the previously beautiful miner's wife is gap-toothed,
standing with her arm around her teenage daughter.
Burnished wood. Willowy. Legend says

that's one tree you should never cut down.
Not even to heat the cabin in an unusual snow.
Not this far south, not this late in the season.

Some of the Lesser-Known Noble Truths

I was walking in the park after snow, the trees were not evenly
burdened. The new dog, rescued and sprung, was running
through them, kicking up powder, working on losing
the path from lost to found so lost was no longer important.
I'm lost most all the time. Over-leashed, un-sprung,
singing under my breath so no one can hear me.
It's been a long winter, I need something to dream.
Allow me to step out on this dead limb
to see if it will hold, see if I can find some small
speck of truth lodged in myself like a splinter.
Let me lay my ear on the cold sill of a propped-open window
and eavesdrop the alcoholics four floors below
on break from their meeting. Truth's got a musky taste,
afterward you'll want a smoke. Tonight everything
looks like smoke, even the moon as it sets
looks like a cup of whiskey set aflame.
Tell me bro, when was the last time you got all fucked up?
When was the last time you sat still long enough to notice
the voices that rise from the iced sidewalk are an uneven
assembly of names called, hands wrung. Splintered yes,
but not wholly undone.

Murmur

This is for the woman in pigtails on the median strip
holding a hand-lettered sign: *Find what you love
and follow it.* It's the day before the vernal equinox
and there's so much standing about in sandals
amidst mounds of discouraged snow, so much
refraction in the cathedral that it's hard to hear
the inner sparrow. The birds come in
on the in-tide and then they're trapped.
There's a man wearing a tee-shirt, logo of
boots and spurs on his chest. Emblazoned.
Like the slash of white
across the muzzle of your favorite horse.
And the couple at the corner table, whispering
into each other's mouth, stroking each other's hands
and cheekbones like there's something hidden there.
There is always something hidden there.
Think of your past as the study of plate tectonics.
Once in the Upper Peninsula in the car of a stranger.
Once beneath a train trestle.
Certain truths abide.
Nobody wants to be the poor in spirit.
Everyone loves a good downpour.

We Dedicate This Practice

to the feeling I've been here before.
Twenty years old, smoking a joint
on the Bridge of Flowers after a night's
exclamatory rain. Yelp of cut grass
and Carl Jung's theory about tigers.
The river flowing beneath the bridge
and the person you are flowing
beneath the surface of yourself
like a river locked in ice but unlocking.
In the ordinary sequence, first it's spring
and the birds are unleashed with their bells.
Then the garden goes berserk.
The heart is a fist-size cup, a watering can
tilting towards asters.
No matter what you can't
extinguish the want. Hush now.
The wind is trying to say something.
It's all become golden and musical.
Like a great polished trumpet,
like a softly blown French horn.
We like to say in the beginning.
Meaning the garden, ourselves in it.
Then comes the travail.
You had no idea how much suffering.
Another beloved, another death
of a beloved in a wooden bed.
Then you're opening doors,
casement windows, anything with a hinge,
saying now I lay me down.
Now I lay me down in a valley,
in a village of thatched roofs,
sidelong in a nest composed of twigs,
stork gone.

Forged

The field where your brother once clubbed a nest of hornets
is now a road besieged by split-levels.
Here's the place in the woods where you found

a stack of National Enquirers, where you read
beneath a beech that a man locked in a sauna became
a human lobster, where you encountered strangeness

surrounded by the complete normalcy of nature.
And you think that has a lot to do with who you are
and how you made your way, found a way out of no way,

the phrase a borrowed one, as so much is.
Borrowed, adapted, someone else's
clothing put on—trouser legs hemmed, jacket let-out,

your hair cut in the style of someone you saw
in a magazine or on a bus lurching down a city street past
graffiti asking basically who the hell are you?

In the next room the dog barks at something
you don't see or hear making the little hairs stand up
on the back of your neck. My neck.

Something is out there in the darkened back yard.
And something is in here, in the darkened
back alleys of your, for lack of a better word, self.

Fusion Frisson

I'm just one sparrow in a flock of sparrows.
One fish in a barrel of fish. I'm a few
nervous disclaimers before the show
but I'm not the show, in no way could I be
mistaken for the show although I have been
known to shake my head and dance.
I've done the shimmy in a barely furnished
bar by the sea and I've done the one-scream
in a stadium of screams but mostly I waltz
alone in a sunny kitchen to the radio,
my moves dedicated to the small hands
on the clock and cubes of sugar all in a row.
I've danced to a few songs sung
through clenched teeth. I've studied a few
centuries of art and the one piece that stays
is a painting of a yellow chair on which
a pigeon perches. Actually, make that two.
There's no arguing with the facts,
there's just no arguing with the facts.
I'll miss you when you're gone, I already
miss the way you button your shirt, standing
before the mirror saying how's this look?
I'll miss the slow unbuttoning
of an afternoon, the great softening of
everything after sex. Think of the shadows
our bodies have made and those thrown
across the lawn when a cloud pauses.
And the blue trumpets of the morning
vining the fence, they herald what—
if not rapture then at least simple joy.

1,000 Cranes

Try standing in the rain until
someone opens a window and sings you in.
A voice like fingertips on the rim of your glass.
Or riding a rusted-out bicycle against the wind,
up a series of increasingly steep hills
just to arrive at your girlfriend's house
as she's slid into the passenger seat
of someone's car, not yours.
It must be Vermont. The winter nights
so long and enduring you'll want
to name them. Then in spring
when the sugar maples begin to weep
and the creek in the backyard spills over
into the basement, more naming.
The house rocking back and forth the way
a person does on her heels when considering.
How much should I tell you?
I've come this far into the story
and now I realize there are too many hills
between setting out and sitting down
unburdened in the middle of the path.
Sing it again! You've got to lay down your sorrows.
You've got to trust in the mind behind your mind.
At the end of the day you've got to
fold your fear into the shape of an animal,
one of your own choosing.
Then set the animal free.
Horses to the pasture, birds to the sky.

While Constellations Dozed

I was licked clean by something incandescent.
Outside my mother's body the white ward.

Outside the ward big-nippled magnolias, milky
month of May. I was well-watered,

I was water from a living well. And no one asked
where from and no one said where to.

Open road was my given name, take me back,
take me way back, was my other.

First kisses, open sesame in a crawl space
beneath the bandstand while the band played,

on the church lawn while inside the priest swayed.
Time was a dreamed moth banging

against the dreamed screen. And then?
What begins as a small tear in the mesh widens.

Lattice crumbles. Bones smolder. Your heart sounds
like a hammer, the night smells like a gun.

Someone forgot to latch the gate and now horses
are running roughshod through the neighborhood.

Beware prized roses, beware unsuspecting travelers
in oncoming cars. Anything worth eating will be.

I Came to See

Yoo-hoo from a dim-lit phone booth—I'm waiting for a call.
My status complicated by stars and stubs
of candles burning between headstones
and the lions mid-yawn at the gate.
I came here to see some chiseled names then missed
the last train home. I thought about walking,
picturing the painting that hung in your hall—
a woman leading a horse across a pasture in a whiteout,
snow cotton-balling their figures.
The foreground, the background.
Then sat down in solidarity with those
for whom this is the last day
with breasts, the heart they were born with, high hopes.
When I get home I need to spend some time
on the couch with my fourth grade self. Dear Diary.
Before I knew the truth I was happy with the myth,
unaware that before the myth was the formless
the undefined, in-the-beginning rants about the dark.
Not cozy sitting in the derelict shed with rusted tools,
mushrooms colonizing the rafters, dark.
Not walking barefooted in wet grass, flashlight
strobing the lawn while my father wrapped a chain
around the storm-split willow, dark. Think open field
subsumed by oaks, bark and phloem taken
first by axe then fire. Fire snuffed. In that order, dark.

Poem Written in Dashboard Dust

There was a town called Goodnight where I didn't sleep,
    couldn't sleep, appaloosas running loose in the street.

Another named Happy where I wasn't.

        There's Muleshoe, Halfway and Zook and some tongue
roughly translated in which *wagga wagga* means
    many crows. There's knowing what we call a thing matters.

Once it seemed a good idea to drive the Buick until
    it ran out of gas then abandon it

right there on a broad saguaro plain
        the range and the ghost-range as our witness.

Once I was twelve. Practicing enactment. I wanted Kansas
    after Oz, little black terrier running for home.

        I wanted to be the funnel cloud
        ripping through aisles of corn.

I thought of my future as the wind, the wind a lasso,
    a coil of rope to be tossed over the neck of the world.

II

Bee Leaves its Stinger

1

Bitter is the tea, enthusiastic the vine
growing up through the seat of the chair.
One bird overhead, riding an updraft &
everywhere I look you're not.
Because there are buzzards in the book
I'm reading I see them everywhere,
in the crow & swan, shadow of cloud.
After a few hours tending the fire
I'm haunted by flames, waves
break against my shale long after
I've driven away from the coast.
Against its will the bee leaves its stinger.
The balloon let loose into the sky
takes a long, slow while to disappear.

2

Everywhere I look you're not.
Not you on the bike whizzing past, not you
ringing your bell, small white dog in the basket
not yours. Not you standing before the movie
marqee having a smoke before the show begins.
Something French & full of easily bruised thighs.
Even on a good day obsessions pile up
like wrecked cars on the freeway in the fog.
What I know about fog is unsettling, obliterating
the lighthouse. So many miles from the sea & still,
I can't stop thinking of it. Right now, I can smell it.
Overhead is a cloud come to remind me of you.
What you used to whistle while cleaning a just-caught
fish. Not the hornpout with their ugly mouths.
But rock bass, striped bass & trout.

3

The balloon let loose into the sky takes a long, slow
while to disappear. One morning, one verb
in declension. Blackberries fat
at the reservoir's lip.
This is the section of road where once
on the downhill coast, feet off the pedals,
I scattered a small herd of horses grazing
on the freedom side of the fence.
No austerity, no measures, no detour
or bridge closures. Red barn doors
unhinged, blown open.

When I Don't Know What Kind of Bird I Am

I'm surprised the mild wind that brought me here
could turn so quickly spooky. Kicked-up, horse-like.

Or, when standing still & I sense myself askew,
at a slight angle to the universe, confused

re. the who & what & how. How to openopenopen.
How to harvest flax without degrading the hills.

The violet and low-rolling hills.
It would help to have a basic understanding

of thermodynamics to better parse, for example,
the ins and outs of heat exchange. As in, it's a cold day

in March, you put your hand in my pocket.
Put your fine, cold hand in my flannel-lined pocket.

It would help if you'd talk a little Bronte, a little Austen
to me while we stroll across the softening fields

to the lambing shed where we'll kneel down
in our muddy boots and count the curly heads.

That Which In Us Rises To Be Sung To

At some point you realize a person can go a long time
between watering holes. Then, like the sorrel mare,
pastured all summer, unfettered, grazing knee-deep
in grass, there is the inevitable looking back
toward the barn with longing. Still, at some point
you may grow weary with your obsessions.
But look—it's the beach and the beach road
paved with broken shells.
The sand and grass and dunes. A shack.
Give me five fingers and I'll look inside.
Am I too heavy? How long can you hold me?
This might be the stage before dying. But we're young,
it's July and we're walking through dunes
which are called parabolic.
Then it's a Monday night and we're at David's place
and it begins to rain. The downpour is calamitous,
dismantling potted plants on the sidewalk.
While the river is rising we sit at a table writing wishes
on scraps of paper then toss them into the flood.
Not oblivious to, but because of. Unencumbered,
our scaffolding disrupted. You're obsessed with hats
and I can't stop thinking about time—cuckoo clocks,
and grandfather clocks with diaphanous winged insects
cruising the dial. This might be the stage before acceptance.
It's best if you hold your arm steady while I look for the vein.
Take the tourniquet into your mouth and think of poppies.
It must be getting late. Someone says:
let me be finished. Another asks: *may I be excused?*
And you owl, for the last two nights, calling,
talons gripping the pine branch outside my window.
Are you complaining or is that plaintive?
Right now I'd give anything to be sung to.

Watch Set to a Time Zone Other Than Home

Let 3 pears in a wooden bowl represent balance,
the freckles of one making up for the lack
of any kind of mark on the other.

Let unbidden, the memory of you
jumping from a pier join with something else—
a single crow rowing its small boat across the sky.

Some of the what-ifs & might-haves lean
like a crooked picket fence. I meant to buy you
flowers but I missed the train. It started to rain

and I was wearing the wrong kind of shoes.
Not knowing how to move a thing forward
is a way. Refusing to struggle with the small

locks of the past, finding your keys don't fit
the door anymore, same thing. Casting the eyes
skyward usually means god help me.

A History of Regret

I think I know what Tolstoy was getting at
leading the couple into the woods,
walking them deeper and deeper in,
the woman kneeling, parting fallen leaves
to get to the white dome of the mushroom,
the hidden and exquisite cap.
But it's been so long since I read the book.
So long since I've seen wildness
on the side of the road or sitting across from me
with its elbows on the table,
I resort to making it up. How far must I go
before I can explicate the forest?
How many days without your hands
sifting through my hair before I dream them?
I didn't mean to leave you stranded
at the bus stop in the rain without an umbrella.
Likewise, the overdose was unintentional.
The flood, I regret the flood and the irreparable
damage to the carpets. Your cats I hope survived.
We survive, move on, but leave something
essential behind, caught on a branch
like fur from the tail of a wild dog.
They say this was once a beautiful boulevard.
Stately elms, overlapping canopy.
Before that it was a cart road
where families walked on Sundays,
babies and concertinas on their hips,
paring knives in wicker baskets and somehow
they knew which mushrooms to cut,
which ones to leave untouched.

Sheep Doth Stray

I can't take my eyes off the ropes and pulleys
yanking the clownish servant across the stage
and what I know about the play itself
could easily fit into the canal of an ear.
An early lover used to do that with his baby finger,
suggestive tickling leading to much arching-over
while outside the room what we didn't know
about living and dying went about its business.
Knowledge of the spinal column has me
hoping the rope will hold.
Perchance you think too much of so much pains?
Perchance, although it's hard to get my mind off
the strange circuitry of cause and effect,
which some say isn't strange but simple. Think seed.
After the seeding of clouds, rain.
After rain the sun comes out like a yeoman
holding a lantern in front of a darkened inn
where tallow lamps burn but a little.
Cease to lament for that thou canst not help.
I can't help myself. I'm not lamenting,
it's just there's so much asking to be picked-up,
saved, plucked from the path of on-coming traffic,
like the perfectly preserved nautilus found
in a land-locked rest stop outside Iowa City.
Or the finely penned letter written on parchment
I pulled from a snow bank that began:
Dear darling, I don't know where to begin.

Early Lessons in Cause and Effect

It's midnight on the train tracks,
the moon has been smoked from the sky
and now, with one hand
on the door of a slow moving freight train
you think about cause and effect.
Your eye on the gap between the ground, your feet
and your blonde half-Cherokee boyfriend
with his hands cupped shouting *lean into it*.
Meaning the iron, meaning the wind.
And later when he comes to your room
by way of the porch roof, his motorcycle cooling
in the maple's huge shadow, you'll lay awake
listening for the lion across town at the zoo
calling most summer nights for that which was
lost in transit, dropped
on the savannah in waist high grass,
or left in the corner of a boxcar —
never delivered to the concrete slab
on the outskirts of Providence
where it paces, measuring the cage.

I Write A Lot Of Letters In My Head

Dear late afternoon sky, dear out-of-the-blue gustiness
stripping the last magenta leaves from the trees.
Dear vortex sniffing about the lone girl
who waits for the bus wearing mittens with buttons for eyes.
Greetings from an imperfectly remembered childhood!
From an old steamer trunk stashed in the attic of a house
where I no longer live. Dear unabridged & uncut,
bootlegged version I've harbored like a fugitive,
complete with barking dogs. Dear self I was at sixteen,
after curfew, beside the unblinking eye of a swimming pool.
Dear John letter begun in haste on the back of a train schedule.
On a lottery ticket. Letter begun in earnest, high-jacked
by self-doubt. Dear veterinarian who kindly euthanized my dog.
Thank you for the donation in his memory.
Dear surgeon who fixed my heart with a piece of mesh,
material Ori imagined as striped like our socks.
Dear container for the uncontainable.
To whom this may concern.

Crush

Start with the boy, the one who moved mid-year
from Fall River. Tattooed stepbrother, a sister who dated.

Make an outline of the summer spent suspended,
swaying in trees—then draw a line through it.

I don't know, I don't remember, I'm afraid to ask.
Years later the boy will be dead. Years later

so much is misshapen, waylaid, outright lost.
If you had to choose one morning

out of all the mornings that have flown
from a lake or lifted from a field burdened with trees,

could you? Not out of fear or lack but on the off-chance
you remember who you are, how you came by

your name. The one your mother chose for you.
The one your father dragged through a clearing

or carried in his arms like a house pet,
hind legs crushed by the wheels of a car.

He put his mouth over its mouth, exchanged
breath for breath.

Broken thing for broken thing.
He said: You'll rise again. You did.

Lying on a Hill Under Stars

None of it is enough.
Not the sheep as they drink
from the millpond
cloven hooves crushing bluets,
the homely thunk of their bells.

Not the blue at the heart of it.

We are like the girl in the rhyme
calling *where o where*,
hands deep in the fleece of ourselves,
wanting someone
with verbena-scented hair
and fine-boned wrists
to lift us up, the whole of us
containable, not yet broken.

Every Day a Deep Drink
from a Hollow Gourd

Every day Exhibit "A" of all that is unknown, unknowable.
A feather falling from an unseen bird caught
in an invisible updraft.
It's time to cover the roses, pluck the last cherry
tomato from the vine. Hard little fruit, not quite red.
Not the arterial red of our hearts but still, bright
enough & illuminated from within
like the paper lanterns I loosely strung
in the East Chop dowager's garden, the summer I left home,
a hired, clumsy girl in an apron given to staring out windows
at the fog settling over the Sound, hearing in the blah-blah
of the horn some version of my name not yet spoken.
Fog the color of the heiress who was each day a little less
here, a ghost in a kimono, stooped at the backyard grave
of her beloved gone dog, the Victrola mascot,
little lop-eared hound of my youth.
These days I stand beneath an oak so big it calls for
a different unit of measure. Feeling smallish. Hen-pecked
by my watch, my heels nipped at by the small, vigilant
collie of my cell phone. Phone which I have placed on silence.
Whose ringer I told not to. I'm thinking about
the leaves that have not yet fallen. Leaves that cling
to the upper branches where the sun is strongest.
All that concentrated, canary-yellow light,
trapped in the tree's interior rooms but still singing.

Dispatch from the Flood

Someone left the gate open and now
woodchucks. Now floodwaters.

There's an *asp* in synapse, there's a wasp
nest hanging on a bough over your head.

The wind is riffling through leaves
as if looking for something lost.

It's August. Green has been taken
to its inevitable conclusion.

There's another high-wind advisory
and you've tried to tie down,

lash to yourself everything in peril.
But the visible is only half the story.

And love, love is racing the fence
like a horse turned out in a storm.

Garrulous As a Crow but Much Larger

After the storm the road is gouged with run-off,

    and the sky turns its back as if fleeing. Like the hermit

who lived behind the sanitarium in a shack, who walked

    with a limp, dragged his bad foot past apple trees

that bloomed but didn't bear fruit. And the man met

    traveling through the States with a backpack,

his English was imperfect, a little off.

    These days it can only be approximated, the place

just east of the continental divide where you slept

    together in a field behind the pool hall.

Finally, that which has roosted in you, garrulous as a crow

    has flown, just barely clearing the roof

of the lame man's shack. Soon enough it will be torn down,

    plowed under, no longer part of this world of salt

and sorrow, including your own which looks more and more

    like the red trim on a Persian rug. Intricately woven

but unfinished, needing to be mule-hauled over

    a few more mountain passes before it's complete.

Poem with an Unknown Number of Wings

I've tried to count the birds inside Bob Marley's voice
but they won't hold still, flying around the red room

of his heart while he sings about redemption.
Across town they're tearing down the asylum.

Soon only the trees will remain and a lawn gone
to seed where patients on furlough used to smoke,

looking up through branches trying to locate the sky.
Two hundred year old oaks, a lawn gone to seed

and the fields—once they were farmed but now
they're running unshackled to the river.

It's got me thinking again about love,
standing before the cave of myself, wishing

I could roll aside the huge stone blocking its entrance.
I'm thinking the birds have grown restless,

that the river would be less without these stones
impeding its flow. It wouldn't look the same,

wouldn't sound the way it does
trying to be heard over my calling from the ruins

of a concrete spillway, asking
is it safe, will it hold me, will it last?

False Spring

So much broken, rusted shut, frozen of gear.
The tin-man's arm forever in mid-chop.
And the spider's nest residing in my own heart
which shall not be untangled, shall not be
plucked and made into a bouquet.
Who said abandon all hope of fruition,
who said anything about fruition?
The world's carriage makes its way home
after dark without benefit of lantern, reaping not
the merit of those who have passed
this way before as it limps across the back pasture
like a hand moving across a page
with its *x*'s and *o*'s, crossed-out false starts,
how-do-you-says. Whatever it is that seems to be
descending, falling down around your shoulders
like rice thrown at a wedding, like dust
from a distant volcano, like a package
dropped from a circling plane, possibly is.

Think Architecturally

When stuck inside the small room of yourself
think architecturally. Find an atrium or skylight.
Likewise, or conversely, when the world looms
a little too large consider some time in the front hall closet
with the hats and umbrellas. Slip your hand in a pocket
and think about warp and weft—
one thread over, one under as a basic unit of measure.
If there's a window to look out of, good.
If there's ivy climbing a brick wall—if it looks back
over its shoulder asking you to keep in touch, better.
Whatever the design, optimistically,
there is always room for improvement.
Always room for expansion, a kitchen re-do,
a sun parlor off the cloudy old one.
Once again I sit here demolished, trying to make
something out of this warped pallet of 2x4's.
Or, here I pace in front of a broken window,
mallet in hand. Looking for connections.
I'm thinking about the settee in grandmother's attic.
Faded rose tapestry, the threadbare
place where the cat slept.
My grandmother's name was Amelia.
She called the cat the Portuguese word for cloud.
Forgive me but I can't right now translate.
I'm trying to think structurally. Get my mind around
buttress, plumb-line and strut.
Trying to get to the concept behind open-plan.

If All Else Fails

Think small. If time allows consider the history
of those tiny horses grazing the steppes of antiquity.
Consider your hat. Break things down into columns:
hats worn, hats lost. The one made of crochet flowers
left on a cross-town bus should stand alone,
the only entry in the category of hats owned for an hour.
Then the people you've loved beneath the hat.
Your father, of course. A man who never went out
without his grey felted man's hat.
Hat with a red feather stuck in its band.
Hat to be worn when all else has failed.
When the glass is not only half empty but broken.
Fedora worn while drinking cheap whiskey.
Hat that cannot tell the difference between
mine and yours. You and me. Two peas, one pod.
Hat donned while making medical breakthroughs
by a woman who works long hours in a lab,
hair tucked-up into something like the skullcaps
used to keep the heads of babies warm.
Cloche-hatted women speaking softly around
a fountain in the square the way our foremothers did,
trading herbs, when not being sold as chattel
or burned at the stake.
Next column, the religious hat.
Hat of the pope and the monk and the novitiate.
Hat to be worn while kneeling in prayer.
Hat to be worn while fleeing your country, all day
and night walking barefoot over mountain passes
thankful for your hat. Because the wind is cold.
Hat to be turned upside-down for collecting alms.
For waving in the air to attract attention, gather
a crowd, punctuate a sermon on realms haunted
by hungry ghosts who, hatless and homeless,
are destined to long for a place to hang theirs.

44

Brief Interlude with Bees

It's good, sitting in a field with a view
of the bay, the water a dazzling multitude
of salt molecules clicking their tiny heels,
mares' tails backstroking across the sky.

Still, I'd like to ask that red-winged bird
what it means speaking from within the tree
then ask the tree to say something for itself.
Let all things speak for themselves.

Let the day wear its big coat with deep pockets,
let it include a rooster crowing from a coop
in the weeds, and card players on folding chairs
smoking beneath the Banyan.

After a day of pillaging the clover
let the honeybee return to the hive.
Sometimes we come home to ourselves
and the larder is empty,

there's music on the stereo but the needle's
stuck playing the same song.
Something something, milk of kindness.
We come home to ourselves, burdened

by the factual—how much, how long
and how many times. No matter the sweetness
we're discouraged by the ratio of nectar to toil.

So Much Potentially Lost in Transmission

The wires downed in a storm,
Volumes I through X
pulled from the shelf and burned.

What you mistook for a rose in the mind
ended up being a cricket kept
in a cage with a small vial of salt.

At dusk a homing pigeon released
into the suede glove of the sky
flies in a circle, marking the four directions.

After a great trauma, after a staggering
loss, there will be a girl wishing
she had something she could tether

beneath a tree. Beyond
the ovens of history, untouched by
the operatic wreckage.

When it's time to go she'll take the slow
way home past backyard plots of corn
and laundry drying on a rope

strung from house eave to fence,
where later, the sound of a carnival
pulled-up for the night in a field of grass

will drift onto the street,
will claim the town, possess it.

Sky Above Is

Snow, the frozen apposite of daisies
tossed from the back of a carriage
has fallen all morning, covering
the courtyard while I sit at a window
trying to locate the tracks I made earlier.
Urgent, compelling and lost.
One, two, three then back to the beginning,
to a field bordered on all sides by stone.
Who was it that time who stood
at the gate then slipped away?
Once three deer emerged from the woods
in a blizzard, watched by a woman
rocking her just awakened baby by a window.
Seeing them appear beneath the huge pine
where crows rafted up, thinking: be careful,
nothing lasts, nothing equals this.
Our bodies are such small countries
connected by water, water everywhere
and still, such thirst.

Field Notes from a State of Well-being

Daybreak along the road
your dog scouting ahead for happiness

and its outposts, the sky
lit like an eggshell held to flame.

The world just the way it is, time
unrolling its silk scroll through you

until you are yourself only younger
there with your first lover

raising yourself like a cup to his mouth
in a room that held only a mattress.

Then memory puts a match to the wallpaper
flowers in your heart, illuminates

yourself quietly leaving another room
where your child sleeps, milk beaded

on her lips, the blue vein in your breast
a coiled rope leading to a great bronze bell,

the moment just before the ringing commences.

III

In Case of Rapture

Beneath the Cape's solid arm there's more water.
Inside magma, magma.
Everything in some way dwelling within something else.
Somehow Buttercup as endearment
has entered the slipstream of language. Somewhere
the assembled fearful are pitching their small tents,
making ready for the coming of The Lord.
Inside the lumpy mattress, coils.
Outside the Truro window, wisteria and oak.
Catbird nagging, saying you, yes you.
Last night I had the smallest dream. No horsemen wrathful
just an old pony whose splayed blonde bangs I brushed
aside. Like always, I wake up thinking about time.
Memory has it that a hand, probably my father's,
fastened my first sunny Timex onto my wrist.
Then gently wound it. Memory allows me
one Bach cantata which I'll whistle later as I sweep.
Why is it I best remember the first and last notes
when what I want is without beginning or end?
Even now I do not believe it.
In the time that remains let me confess.
Once I stole a woman's cashmere coat.
Once my boyfriend and I broke into an empty summer
cottage. I lifted the window and let him enter first.
In a big bed in a small room we found a way but forgot
to fashion a return. When he left me
I knew what the scientists meant by hollow collapse
of stars. That deepest part of the ocean they call the lightless,
the abyssal plain. In another dream I went house to house
checking every door. Big sound of nothing.
Along the whole stretch of beach not a soul was home.
That, or they were home but couldn't hear me.
They were home but couldn't bring themselves to answer.

Counting the Immeasurables

One, the garden gate frozen in place.
Two, you have no idea how to fix it.
Meanwhile your heart has been broken into,

is a jigsaw puzzle of a moonlit field
with a lone tree at its center, the tree struck
by lightning and split down the middle.

It's night but there's so much unfiltered
light falling from the moon you can see grass
moving on the slope of the hill below you, moving

in waves as if underwater. You'd like to
say something true, but the truth seems so multiple,
stratified. It's hard to make out the voice

running like a bass line in the wind,
or the one trying to be heard from within
the waves throwing themselves

against the wooden pylons of a pier
in the seaside town where you no longer live.
Three, you no longer live near the sea.

A Small Glitch at the End of a Bloodline

It's the day after a two-day blizzard
and the citizens are out surveying.
Heft of shovel, they're walking
down the middle of unplowed roads
clutching each other. Newly arrived
I'm sitting in a parked car on Hope St.,
listening to ska. Earlier I crossed Benevolence,
honked as I ran the light on Hazard.
What am I to make of a city
whose intersections are so morally instructive
under a sky that seems to feel okay
about losing its stuffing?
O survivors. O shaved head,
tattoos up and down the arms.
We build the temple then we burn it down.
In roughly the time it takes to strike a match
you might be stricken from the record.
I'd give anything to see you again,
to sit with you on the steps of the cathedral
while the choir practices lamentations,
our backs against the portico, hands open
to the back and forth sparrows
who are small of wing, big of heart.

Letter Written in this Life,
Mailed from the Next

When I say I want to go back I mean the beach,
waking up on the sand after driving
all night in my brother's car.
Or the hillside Shinto shrine where years later
I lost my favorite dungaree jacket.
It's always a summer night and I'm standing
at the threshold of something unstoppable —
1st sex against the marble plinth in the cemetery,
hand-rolled cigarettes behind the crypt.
Love and death, hand-rolled and licked.
I mean little blue budgie before the storm hit,
still swinging on his bamboo perch,
or the picture I used to keep tacked above my desk:
2 donkeys leaning against each other
in the arched threshold of a stone hut.
Necks entwined. Looking left, looking right.
I mean the places where we've been rendered
helpless, stranded in each other
like turtles who come to the sand-spit to lay eggs
but turn away because there's not enough
eelgrass to cover their tracks.

One Less Sparrow

Sheep dotted the hillside, the electrified fence
for once was turned off. I lost my favorite
necklace on a hummocky slope
then spent the next week on my knees
trying to find it. Once I made love to a man
while his long-time girlfriend sat
outside the bedroom door loudly weeping.
Calling his name. Nearly or dearly
besotted, how much cruelty is too much?
And what gesture too small?
There's something I've been meaning
to tell you becomes I brought you some
flowers. The hawk dive-bombing the lilac
means there's one less sparrow in the world.

Photo Enclosed

Here I am, practicing receptivity,
palms up in the universal gesture of
gimme-gimme asked nicely.

And here, reclining in a pasture
with my boots kicked off.
I used to think it would be easy

to break love down, punch it
into bite-sized verb-noun clusters.
Parse & parsimony.

But having walked all the way
across town for a chanced glimpse
of your silhouette in the window,

your apartment framed by
those towers & cables, the bridge
be-strung at twilight, huge

bulbs projecting mega-wattage
& the river below bird-plain,
I discover I can't.

Woe & Whoa

I'm standing in a phone booth trying to read
faded ink on a scrap of paper
while the carousel at the end of the pier spins

so fast and out of whack
it's hard to tell if the horses are happy.
Along comes the wind.

Our planet is wobbling like a kicked toy,
like an overburdened cart heaped
with the fruit of all desire and rotting.

The fires we've been
building to lessen our darkness
have jumped the tracks, slipped their harnesses,

flame joining hands with flame, walking
in ruby slippers across the lawns of our neighbors—
goodbye split-level, goodbye mobile home,

desert tents, tasseled rugs, tea glasses—
Look, our animals are scattering, the herd dispersed.
The red in their eyes is equal to the dust rising

behind them and in front of them
so you can't tell which comes first,
the stampede or the cloud.

Coat As Metaphor

Rock, paper, scissors, I wore it to shreds
then left it on a pier in P-Town the spring
I turned seventeen, a season best remembered
as the curb outside the factory
where my father worked,
where I sat, elbows on knees,
because I couldn't bring myself to enter.
And the street corner in the center of town remains
the place where I waited after school for a boy,
the first to lift my chin so he could kiss me.
A freight train came through every night, late.
I used to listen for it at my window as I smoked
the day's last cigarette, some nights
so quiet you could hear leaves dropping
like buttons from the front of the coat
when the stitching let go.

Fractious Pastoral

I go walking in the early morning mudflats
of your eyes. In electric, 12-string feedback
squawk of gulls. Fervent and without a coat,
without the necessary arrangements.
In this way I'm like the girl hitch-hiking
on a back road where not much traffic happens.
Where the first spring dandelions on the hill
beneath the penitentiary are sacred.
I go walking after midnight when
the houses of my neighbors are stove-black dark
and every other sound has been extinguished
like the small fire that leaps
from one stack of dried straw to another
before dying out. Again and again
in the hour of betrayal, first light breaking
its promises, I go walking.
And it's not winter or spring or summer
but all of these conjoined. And the moon
is not a mistress or a lantern hung
on the branch of a tree but a planet, a mighty
influence at the confluence
of night into day and vice versa. It makes me
punch-drunk rising over the Great Swamp
where spring frogs by the gazillion
shake their little lives. Shake them because
it's all that they've got. Shake them like a fan-dancer
doing the can-can on a rough built stage.
Bells on her fingers, bells on her toes.

When You Realize There's No Going Back

You're in an alley between teashops
looking for the door of the fan maker
in a city of streets named according to
which tree, which season.
The plum is *ume* which is your daughter's name
in smoke. She's not born yet, not even conceived
although she will be soon, this afternoon
of rain, after which cumulus clouds
will come out to nibble the season's first greens.
There's a cafe whose name is *Time Paradox*
but the slant of the letters makes it look like *Lime*
and now it's best remembered incorrectly.
And the old man peddling his bicycle
through the temple yard
is bringing home the day's tofu.
You're trailed by the scant ringing of his bell.
Leaves blowing around the shrine
to the Backward Glancing Bodhisattva are
the color of the next world's apples.

A Little Rue

When I die, put me in a casket in the shape of a lion
or a tooled blue marlin with a bill as long as my arm.
Then lay me down and let the savannah go on without me.
In the sea with the plankton and weeds.
Or put me in a clay pot but let me have always before me
the rooftops of Paris as seen from a rooftop in Paris
so I can keep my eye on the boulevards
and little, cobbled Rue Du-Chat-qui-Peche, a place
I knew nothing about until the summer my love moved in,
a little rue falling from his mouth as he read to me in bed,
words he explained then didn't, falling like fruit
from a vendor's cart, chilled in the air off the Seine.
Take this, my final request spoken in a poor smattering
of French then give me the Seine and the Somme and a river
somewhere else called the Po. Excusez moi, not just the river
but its bank crowded with hawkers and gliders,
a pierced couple dancing the oblivion tango, pantomime
in white stripes miming a baby finding her face in a spoon.
Give me muddy flotsam, stinky jetsam, the whole
blameless and flaming sun parade. Let it include
grown-ups playing hide and seek, taking cover behind
lamp posts and statues, taking refuge with the broken
noses and split torsos of antiquity in a garden
once famously tulipped.

Rare Blue

Most mornings the man sitting on a milk crate
in front of Haymarket Juice Joint will, for spare change,
quote Rilke: *das ist ein fluch.* Got anything for me today?

Although my mind is on fire it's nothing
when compared to the flash of the rare blue butterfly,
habitat reduced to the shadowed air beneath a defunct

train trestle in the Keys, or a version tattooed on the nape
of the runaway's neck. Yes, I've walked the length
of Atlantic Ave. in the rain. Yes, I've swum beneath the pier,

the off-season ocean closed, boarded-up like a parts plant.
But when did it happen that one last stroll
through an abandoned vineyard became a way of life?

Grapes too heavy for the vine, vines bringing the trellis down.
I loved a boy like that once. After a night on the beach
I loved him for the way he emptied everything

from his pockets, tossed it all into the surf
and his devotion which he spoke so sweetly, lisping
through chipped teeth whenever he said my name.

Possibly Cello

Happiness is a window seat at the Blind Spot Café
where I sit at a table with a bit of a wobble, spilled

sun on my face and thighs, a warmth reminding me
of a particular boy, a certain afternoon arriving

unexpectedly when we pulled each other through
the small opening we'd established in heaven

with words, his voice a cross between the pigeons
crooning in the high rafters of my uncle's barn

and the bass treble of a large stringed instrument,
possibly cello. Likewise I've come to believe

in the unbidden, the not-searched-for—and today,
all that is innermost wants out, the petals of the lotus

relaxed, pink tips brushing the surface of the swamp
and there's only a thin stalk between me

and the likelihood of flight.

4th of July, Girl Jumping
from Abandoned Railroad Bridge

Having climbed the iron trestle she stood
in her bra and panties to declare
her love in the face of a swift current
for the boy idling just downstream in a motorboat,
shifting her weight from one hand to the other
50 feet above the river, considering the plunge,
saying to herself but loud enough
so onlookers can hear: *i can do this i can do this.*
Then, against the kiln of the sky and the arc
of river bank she leaned forward, stepped
away from the bridge, her feet on the first rung
of the air's blue ladder.
I'm trying to remember what it felt like,
leaping like that. When my hands left the rail,
when I rested them on your face
or the small of your back, speaking your name
as I fell, not into cold river water, but still, falling
like when we're born or dying in a dream,
the seasons out of order: the winter we met,
snow obliterating monuments in the cemetery
becomes the summer we prayed for rain
becomes the spring that the rain
just wouldn't stop.

Driving Home From The Zendo

On the side of the road a small herd of deer stand
with their ears raised listening to a truck pass
and in my mind are still there two days later
grazing in the dark. Their necks outstretched
like God's arm, like God reaching for his pipe,
having a smoke with his world of fault
lines and phosphorus, wind-swept peninsulas,
tumbleweeds blowing across a town square at dusk.
Meanwhile the deer continue to exemplify
the discipline of practice and my mind wanders
so far afield in big sky country it's no longer in it.
On the radio the usual programming is interrupted
with news that in July the moon is called thunder.
Then, another staticky interlude in which
a museum guide speaks of beauty and its possession;
a painting in oil of a horse with tangled mane
leaning its heaviness against a gate's split rail,
flanks heaving as if there were another caught inside.
The way a person might regard a tree while speeding,
going a few miles over the speed limit and thinking
maple or *aspen* because those are the given words
but meaning something more akin to *tiger* or *silver*.
Meaning the terraced mine from which it is hauled.
Including the backs of men as they strain to lift it
and the deer who stand with their ears pressed forward
in the universal language of the burst-upon,
the suddenly awake—open
like the flue of a chimney or cactus flowers,
so thin and fine and papery
the headlights of on-coming cars shine through.

Watching You Leave in a Hail Storm

for Elizabeth

I'm standing on the roof of the airport garage
while below me in the harbor a sailboat
tacks in and out of fog.
On the tarmac a 747 is tuning up
and men in orange jump-suits load luggage
like workers packing the hive.
It's comforting to think of bees
while staring down from the concrete roof
of an airport at machinery too big, even for the sky.
Hail the size of a child's fist falling at my feet.
I'm going to stay here until you leave,
long enough to mention the flowering tree
we've stood beneath, taking turns
saying *don't go, come with me.*
During the day the bees work that tree
like it's a switchboard, and then at night
the moon bends down and cools it, each petal,
each blown and emptied socket.

Poem with a Shaft of Light Running Through It

It's the first day of autumn and the light is so
quickly running out, it's loping across the afternoon
like a fox in a field of grass.
Just yesterday I lay down in that grass
and made an imprint of myself
while my mother called my name
from a back porch, backlit by grief.
And you, how long has it been since someone called
your name from a porch as street lights came on,
warming the road? How long since birds
assembled in its branches?
Now it seems even the street has forgotten you.
No longer listening for the sound of your shoes
coming home late from the library,
maple and ash leaves falling on your shoulders
or later, in another season, snow swirling
around you in big pieces like pages
torn from a book where your name has been
written, erased, written again.

Absinthe Makes the Heart

I'm waiting for the bus to Providence,
bouquet of asters in hand, the usual
thunder in the occiput, and next to me
a girl with tattooed glyphs on her cheek,
some kind of dangerous-sounding funk
seeping from her headphones.
Boom-chucka-boom sister, we're all
pilgrims. Sometimes we're incandescent,
sometimes our filaments are embarrassingly
visible. Think of geese v-ing overhead, the sun
illuminating their shabby undercarriages
or the way a small slat of light slips
beneath the door, illuminating dust bunnies.
Whatever it is you're drinking
I love the soft glug as you pour it
from the bottle stashed in your backpack.
And I love, don't you, that our spirits may be
shook until what was clear clouds over,
reduced to the thujones, and yet,
whatever remains remains aloft.

When Big was Huge

It's snowing, flakes flying like marble chunked
from the monstrous-thighed gods of Late Antiquity,

back when big was huge and we're skittering down
the hill in the back pasture with the dog who can't keep up

because he can't resist the drifts, now he's rolling, now
he's inching along on his back in the snow.

There ought to be more glee in this world especially
with so many of its lamps turned low, sputtering.

And more ghee offered to the gods as appeasement.
Rarefied and sanctified, an aspiration

to which we would adhere, like the snow
sticking to our lashes. Meaning please allow us

one more day in the orchard with the past season fruit
dried and clinging to bare branches and that blessed break

between trees that lets us see all the way into town,
the steeples and spires looking like party hats.

Because we do love the view. And while you're at it
grant us sufficient distance, an aperitif to our daily bread,

so we may see it. Let even the sound of the wrecking ball
thwacking the walls of the asylum next door

seem far away, removed,
like the look that comes over you my love,

your gaze softening, your eyes little dove cotes
when the birds have flown.

On Being Asked to Imagine
the World's Last Lark

The best I can do is hover above it, the thought, my wings
tucked to keep myself
clear of the concrete, the paved-over,
that which lacks backwater, bracken and peat.
Besides, I can't take my eyes off the two girls rolling
in each other's arms, yipping like small undomesticated dogs
apparently not noticing the long shadows
moving across them and the library lawn.
I'm only hovering over it, unlike the girls who've dug in,
spread their purple blanket, spilled themselves
like a bag of apples on top of un-swept leaves,
unstable, nothing like the red flower of the sturdy
geranium, its face pressed against the glass of the south wing—
and not swift either, no comparison
to the fleet of scooters streaming by
nor nimble like the one girl
putting something into the opened mouth of the other,
something small that she's holding between her fingers
which from this distance can only be imagined as sweet.

Dear Asteroid, Dear Beehive

The bay has risen to meet me and finally,
after much ado I've been inducted

into the discipleship of fog. The queen's roses
are incandescent at dusk, likewise

the fused spark in the carriage hack's eye.
Not much has changed.

I still startle when the hawk leaves my wrist
and after startle comes umbrage.

Like the song says:
if you want me I'll be in the bar.

Endeared and engorged and yet, in a while
none of this will matter. Not the honeybee

in the weedrack, not starfish abandoned by the tide.
Nor the series of plaster of Paris statues

I've done in your likeness
and set on the lawn to dry.

Notes

"Disturbed Cirrus" is a meteorological term coined by poet Karen Donovan and was written under the influence of her poem "From a Catalogue for a Colorist."

"The Use of Sorrow to Overcome Sorrow" was overheard in a conversation between two blues musicians in describing what they do.

In "Sheep Doth Stray" the lines "perchance you think too much of so much pains" and "cease to lament for that thou canst not help" are from *Two Gentleman of Verona.*

"Fractious Pastoral" was inspired by the poetry of Sean Janson. The line "fervent and without the necessary arrangements" is from "Sometimes" by Mary Oliver.

"Fusion Frisson" owes its genesis to Michael Pettit's *Ones-Self, En-Masse.*

Acknowledgments

This book is the result of enormous amounts of love, support and friendship from the following people: The Emerging Writers of the North Shore: David "The Mayor" Byer, Leni Gross Young, Allison Lobdell, Lynn Stevens, Elizabeth Slade: in perpetuity writing wishes on paper and tossing them into the flood. The Fairview Writers: Elissa Alford, Markie Babbott, Elisabeth Slade, Kristen Stake: long may we howl. The Big Girls Po Group: Annie Boutelle, Amy Dryansky, Diana Gordon, Mary Koncel, Carol Potter, Margaret Szumowski and Ellen Watson. Gratitude to my faculty advisers at Warren Wilson College, with special thanks to Betty Adcock, Steve Orlen, Martha Rhodes and Eleanor Wilner. Thank you to Steve Strimer and Diana Gordon of Hedgerow Books for their generosity and unwavering support. And my family—the perfect pod!

Author

MAYA JANSON received her BA from Smith College, her MFA from Warren Wilson College, and has been a recipient of an artist fellowship from the Massachusetts Cultural Council.

She lives in Florence, Massachusetts and is employed as a community health nurse and a lecturer in poetry at Smith College.